W9-DAU-259

EXPECT NOTHING
A ZEN GUIDE

EXPECT NOTHING
A ZEN GUIDE

CLARICE BRYAN

JOURNEY EDITIONS
BOSTON • TOKYO • SINGAPORE

This edition published in 2001 by Journey Editions, an imprint of Periplus Editions (HK) Ltd., with editorial offices at 153 Milk Street, Boston, Massachusetts, 02109.

Copyright © 2001 Clarice Bryan

All rights reserved. No part of this publication may be reproduced or utilized in any form or by any means, electronic or mechanical, including photocopying, recording, or by any information storage and retrieval system, without prior written permission from Journey Editions.

Library of Congress Cataloging-in-Publication Data
Bryan, Clarice
    Expect Nothing: A Zen Guide / Clarice Bryan.
        p. cm.
    Includes bibliographical references.
    ISBN: 1-58290-039-6
        1. Religious life—Buddhism. 2. Religious life—Zen Buddhism. I. Title.
BQ5395 .B69 2001
294.3'444—dc21   00-055562

Distributed by

North America   Japan
Tuttle Publishing   Tuttle Publishing
Distribution Center   RK Building, 2nd Floor
Airport Industrial Park   2-13-10 Shimo-Meguro, Meguro-Ku
364 Innovation Drive   Tokyo 153 0064
North Clarendon, VT 05759-9436   Tel: (03) 5437-0171
Tel: (802) 773-8930   Tel: (03) 5437-0755
Tel: (800) 526-2778
Fax: (802) 773-6993

Asia Pacific
Berkeley Books Pte Ltd
5 Little Road #08-01
Singapore 536983
Tel: (65) 280-1330
Fax: (65) 280-6290

Designed by Dutton & Sherman

05 04 03 02 01 00   9 8 7 6 5 4 3 2 1

Printed in the United States of America

THIS BOOK IS DEDICATED TO MY MOTHER, CLARICE DAVIS ZION, WHO, WHILE APPRECIATING AND ENCOURAGING ALMOST EVERYTHING, EXPECTED NOTHING. I WISH I'D REALIZED THIS WHILE SHE WAS STILL ALIVE.

CONTENTS

ACKNOWLEDGMENTS

I gratefully acknowledge the many people who have contributed in so many ways to my life and the writing of this book.

I extend special thanks and my great respect to my teachers, Thich Nhat Hanh and Sogyal Rinpoche, who are unaware of their great influence on me. I am deeply grateful for encouragement and support from Lynn Warner and Phyllis Wilner. I extend my very special thanks to Patsy Givins, whose editorial advice has been extremely valuable to me. I offer heartfelt appreciation to Jan Johnson and Robyn Heisey of Tuttle Publishing for their excellent guidance.

INTRODUCTION

How do we act in the world? How do we call forth the world without harming ourselves, other people and the world itself? How do we carry as little baggage as possible into each moment, and accumulate as little baggage as possible in each moment? How do we enter into each moment of the present with a clear conscience and a clear consciousness, gently holding and realizing the world and our life?

*Richard Baker**

I'm just a beginning Buddhist, but in trying to grasp the meaning of not grasping, I have found an intermediate

---

step of not expecting. Seek and ye shall find . . . ask and it shall be given—more and more expectations everywhere you look. I have spent much of my life being distracted by what could be.

I have been the great expecter!

Putting expectations on myself is one thing, but putting expectations on others is a travesty. I burden someone else with my needs for their behavior. I create unneeded and usually unwanted goals for others and then expect them to understand my disappointment and sometimes my anger when they don't live up to my goals. It is really my expectations that fail, not the other people, but, of course, I blame them.

I have been a rabid perfectionist most of my life. I practiced perfection. I expected everything I did to be perfect, and I expected everything everyone else did to be perfect—by my standards of perfection, of course, not theirs.

Slowly, I am learning that people are different—especially that they are different from me. They have different time concepts, different food preferences, different religions, different cultural behaviors, different politics, and talents, and philosophies.

One of my own philosophical differences is that I happen to agree with the teachings of Buddhism. A friend once said it takes years to put one's philosophical beliefs into action. Putting my beliefs into action is what I am working on here.

Certainly it is through our actions that we are known. But do we act the way we are or the way someone expects us to act?

Act like a woman. Act like a man. Act like an adult. Act like a professional. Pretend to be something others expect you to be, even if you're not.

Usually these are the rules of society. Sometimes they are someone else's idiosyncratic expectations.

As living beings, we have been given so many miracles, yet we seem to continue to expect more and more of ourselves, of everyone else, and of the planet.

Writing this manuscript is one way for me to come to terms with the knowledge and principles of the Buddhist discipline. This is a philosophy that brings me peace and joy, and I hope to share it with others. I believe that we can live better if we expect less in every aspect of our lives.

It doesn't matter what you've been given, whether it's physical deformity or enormous wealth or poverty, beauty or ugliness, mental stability or mental instability, life in the middle of a madhouse or life in the middle of a peaceful silent desert. Whatever you're given can wake you up or put you to sleep. That's the challenge of now: what are you going to do with what you have already— your body, your speech, your mind?

Pema Chodron

PART I
TEACHERS

Each of us encounters many teachers in our lifetime. We don't always know that they are our teachers at the time, this awareness only coming later. Even a rock can be a teacher, after all. As I move more deeply into Buddhism, I see that I have been blessed with good teachers all around me, though it has often taken me too long to glean their lessons. We are surrounded by teachers, if only we know enough to see them. One way to acknowledge and truly own the lessons life has for us is to identify and acknowledge the teachers of those lessons. Here are some of mine.

ONE

JUST LIVING

*Our lives are lived in intense and anxious struggle, in a
swirl of speed and aggression, in competing, grasping,
possessing, and achieving, forever burdening ourselves
with extraneous activities and preoccupations.*

Sogyal Rinpoche

During my past life, one of expecting everything, I made
some adjustments in the way I lived. Many things were
reduced to the level of automatic responses.

I expected the alarm clock to go off when I set it, and
as a result of storms and electrical outages, I purchased a
windup alarm clock.

I expected there to be coffee and toast available for
breakfast. That's why I made a grocery list and bought
stuff before it ran out.

I expected to have cleaned, ironed clothes ready to put on before I left the house. That's why I washed and ironed them ahead of time.

I expected the car to start and have gas in it. So I filled it ahead of time and took it to the mechanic before it fell apart.

I had all these expectations. They weren't met, for a variety of reasons—from relying on electric alarm clocks to being too tired to shop or being just plain forgetful.

But now, I really don't expect any of these things. And I get an interesting surprise when other things happen—though I still have a windup clock.

Most of us have been through all these failures of expectations and these changes, and now, usually, most things go according to our expectations, at least those things that are within our own control and grasp. Control and grasp are so full of expectation, commitment, and energy, they seem as if they belong to the very core of life.

When other people get involved, like spouses, children, parents, friends, and strangers, even more disastrous events can take place.

The morning paper didn't get delivered on time. Somebody drank all the milk. Somebody else didn't get up in time to get to school without a ride.

The slow driver in the fast lane. So many cars on the road at this hour. The secretary is late again, and my tests aren't ready. The lecturer assigned for today's session thought it was scheduled for tomorrow. Two of the three committee members didn't do their homework, so we had to postpone the meeting.

Other people just don't seem to understand how hard I work, and that is why they fail to do what I need at the right time. Other people just don't understand my simple concepts. Other people are involved in too many other things, instead of *my* things.

Or worse—other people are mean and vindictive. They don't respect me. They come from a different planet. It's all their fault I don't get my work done and don't get promoted.

There are only two alternatives here that I see:

1. If I want it all done right, I must do it all myself, which creates too much work and too many expectations in my already burdened life.

2. Expect nothing, which also happens to free and liberate me and bring me peace and joy. Of course, expect nothing takes much less energy. And it also frees other people and me from myself.

To release means to release mind from its prison of grasping, since you recognize that all pain and fear and distress arise from the craving of the grasping mind.
Sogyal Rinpoche

TWO

ONE OF MY GREATEST TEACHERS

Let none find fault in others. Let none see omissions and commissions in others. But let one see one's own acts, done and undone.

Dhammapada, verse 50

John came to live with me after his father, my brother, died. John didn't get along well with anyone but his father. John had been diagnosed as schizophrenic, though not violent nor terribly disabled, just socially different. He had finished high school, and he'd lived at home all his life. He was now in his forties. I have a little studio house on my property, so it seemed logical that he should move in with me. And that's where he lives.

John has a fantastic memory, especially for numbers and dates. He's a *Star Trek* fanatic and forever tries to tell anyone who will listen about some of his favorite stories—from years back or last night's show. And he can recall these stories in great detail, which I assume is accurate. He has *Star Trek* cards, buttons, books, and he even goes to *Star Trek* conventions. Fortunately, I like *Star Trek,* but not all the time.

He also has some fundamental knowledge of cars, house repair, and carpentry, although it's often not appropriate to the situation at hand. After several minor disasters, involving broken hoses in the engine of my car, fingers nearly cut off, goats eating the flowering plants instead of their own, tools and equipment left out to rust, and stuffing up the attic air vents in the belief that he could make the house warmer, we now talk about each project beforehand. We see what will work and what won't. Even so, I often need to supervise closely. John would never make a good cat burglar because he never puts things back where he finds them. I can trace his every move.

John is generous and polite. He bathes and takes care of his clothes. And he means well, which is probably why we get along. Sometimes he gets a fixed idea of what should be done, and no matter how I try to convince him of the errors of his logic, he will often go ahead and muck something up anyway. But sometimes he is right, so I listen.

When he first came, I tried to make him part of my family. I didn't charge him for room or board, but I did expect him to do things that needed doing by a strong man, which he is. I expected him to water the garden sometimes, but he was too inconsistent about it for most plants to do well. I expected him to weed, but that didn't work at all. We rototilled and planted a vegetable garden for him to take care of and call his own. It soon became a marvelously thick green growth of tall weeds. I expected him to help me put up some fencing for the goats, which he did, but with much moaning and groaning.

In fact, moaning and groaning accompanied any hard physical labor. He helped me enclose the front porch so we now have a sun and plant room, but there was plenty of wailing and gnashing of teeth. I did not feel good when he moaned and groaned. I did not feel good when he failed to do something easy that I asked him to do.

I wanted him to find some way to develop self-respect, because he could do many things, just not always at the right time or place. I kept trying to think of things he could do that might ultimately lead to a job or productive output. I knew his father had taught him a lot about bricklaying, but he didn't want to have anything to do with that.

He'd already tried classes at his own community college, apparently without success. So those suggestions went nowhere.

I tried to interest him in making copies of my bird feeder, which has a beautiful oriental design, so he could reproduce it and sell it to local nurseries, but that never got off the ground.

I offered to buy a premade, do-it-yourself little barn that he could put together for when and if we have miniature donkeys, but he was not thrilled with the idea.

He must have thought I was the aunt from hell.

To keep the goblins from making a mess out of my stomach when he didn't meet my expectations, I quit having expectations. It didn't look as if I could change him, so I would have to change me.

Now I charge him rent, though not board, but I only feed him dinner and snacks. He has a kitchen of his own. And now he can choose to do some of my chores or not. I pay him $6.00 per hour when he decides to. When he decides not to, which is often, I hire a graduate student, who is much more efficient and knowledgeable, for $10.00 per hour.

I cook dinner and he does the dishes, which he leaves all over the kitchen counters, even though he knows where they belong. He will weed-eat the lawn edges about once a month, take the garbage up to the street once a week—most of the time. He'll even clean the goat barn sometimes. He records TV shows he knows I like when I'm going to miss them, often *Star Trek*.

And now my stomach is happy. I'm happy. In many ways, I do live close to Nirvana, not just in my dealings with John, but by applying my John-learning to everything else. And I think John is happier, too. His aunt found her way out of hell and into his real world, such as it is. We get along well and understand each other's failings.

I have quit trying to make John into all I think he could be—or even some of what I think he could be. He may already be all he can be. That's not for me to know, let alone expect.

The Tibetan Buddhists believe that there is no greater vehicle than compassion and forgiveness to counteract suffering caused by the self-grasping attitude.

Dalai Lama and Phil Borges

THREE

GROWING UP

*We do not "come into" this world; we come OUT of it as
leaves from a tree. As the ocean "waves," the universe
"peoples." Every individual is an expression of the whole
realm of nature, a unique action of the total universe.*

                                                    Alan Watts

I was fortunate growing up. I had a close, loving mother
and a distant, but tolerant father. Both parents worked,
and, as a result, we often had my grandmother or my aunt
at home with my two older brothers and me.

Looking back, I think my parents did the most important
thing parents can do for their children. They empowered us.
I was allowed and encouraged to do lots of things. Until I was
nine, we lived in San Francisco on Twin Peaks, a long way
from the center of town. I remember hiking to the streetcar

on Market Street and taking it to my mother's office at the waterfront. She was a secretary for the Department of Agriculture. When I went to her office, we would go to lunch, and then I would go back home on the streetcar.

We all hiked a mile or so to school, and after school I went to Mrs. Drew's for piano lessons, returning home on foot. In those early years, not much was expected of me, and I did what I did with no expectations for myself either. I especially did not expect to become a concert pianist.

As far as my culture's expectations were concerned, I was too tall and too athletic. And, God forbid, when I was twelve and couldn't read the stuff on the blackboard anymore, I had to wear glasses. So I had to work a bit harder than those who were the right size, who were fragile enough to be thought feminine, and who could see. I'm sure they had their own problems, because our culture doesn't allow anyone to feel truly secure about appearance, even Ingrid Bergman.

When I was nine, my dad retired from working for the City of San Francisco and could now live outside the city limits, so we moved to San Mateo, twenty miles south of San Francisco. Dad was sixty when I was born. He didn't retire until he was sixty-nine, because most of his friends who retired earlier seemed to die too soon. Mom was eighteen years younger than Dad and still worked and commuted to San Francisco. Now that my dad was around all day, he had expectations.

We bought a big old house, much in need of repair, and while my brothers helped Dad with the electrical, plumbing, and building stuff, I became chief house painter and gardener. And what a sloppy painter and gardener I was. I heard about it every day that summer. Though I did get better at painting and gardening, returning to school was a blessed relief.

Since my mother worked, I was also chief house cleaner, ironer, and kitchen aide. Mom preferred to be chief clothes washer (we had no electric washer or dryer) and chef. Perhaps she had tried me out on these and decided it was best to do them herself. I don't remember. But I did develop some competencies and some positive self-esteem.

When I was sixteen, my dad said, "You're old enough to get married now without our permission. I expect you to find someone as soon as you can." But Mom said, "You can always get married. Live your own life first." So I did.

Dad blamed the cod-liver oil I was fed as a kid for making me as tall as he was. He really wanted me to be petite, lovely, a good pianist, a good seamstress, and married. In some ways I'm sorry I did not live up to my father's expectations, but I'm sure I'm more me now than if I had accepted his expectations as my own.

Fortunately, at that young age, I had a pretty good idea about what was me and what was not me, so I could make the choice.

A child's world is fresh and new and beautiful, full of wonder and excitement. It is our misfortune that for most of us that clear-eyed vision, that true instinct of what is beautiful and awe-inspiring is dimmed and even lost before we reach adulthood.

Rachel Carson

FOUR

ANIMALS

Animals are here in part to grant glimpses of the grace of beauty.

Matthew Fox

Having five cats around the house helps me have no expectations. They are not goal-fulfilling creatures in any human sense. There is little one can expect of a cat.

Whenever I have a cat on my lap, I am able to look at it as a remarkable being with perfect markings, perfectly formed nose and eyes, and delightful ears, and I am always awed at such perfection even though each cat is different. Even their very strange unique characteristics seem perfect to me: six toes, lopsided coloring, scars, deafness, odiferous moments. I am satisfied and expect nothing more. Why don't I feel this way with humans?

I do expect to get bopped by any cat that I do not pet mindfully. Each cat's likes and dislikes are different, so mindful petting saves me a lot of scratches and bleeding. If I am not paying attention to their needs they have effective means of getting my attention. They are patient about learning my strange ways of communicating, so I try to be patient learning theirs.

At the moment, I don't have a dog myself, yet when I see someone walking on the street with a dog, I always look at the dog. Just seeing a dog is satisfying in itself. When I drive by a field where there are any newborn animals—calves or kids or foals—I can't help but smile and feel good. My pygmy goats have been a delight. They are full of affection and playfulness, without being aggressive or mean.

When I look at all these animals, I see Buddhists in action. They are mindful of all that is around them and of their every action. They appear to expect nothing, except for the few feeding habits I've forced upon them. They've taught me patience and love, mindfulness and compassion. They've taught me the value of learning as much as I can about them so that I can enjoy them even more.

There's a cat sitting on the top of this page at this moment as I write this at the dining room table. There are muddy cat prints on several pages of this manuscript.

Animals teach us that one can be sensual and spiritual at the same time. They know that abstractions by themselves, such as money for example, are not what living and ecstasy are about.

Matthew Fox

FIVE

CATS AND BIRDS

We cannot fix the world, we cannot even fix our own life. By accepting failure we express our willingness to begin again, time after time. By recognizing failure we change, renew, adapt, listen, and grow. It is only by participating without expectation of success that we can ever truly open to the world, to suffering and to joy.
                                        Thich Nhat Hanh

I do love cats. I love birds, too. Their markings are as amazing as those of a cat.

I have a large bird feeder atop a ten-foot metal pole. The metal pole prevents climbing creatures from climbing up to it. I do have to use a ladder to refill the feeder, but that's kind of fun.

It is hard to have a wild kingdom in your own back-yard, because not all beasts are as gentle as the goats. Cats are known to catch birds, and when they do, they usually bring them to me . . . which, I guess, is a good thing.

This morning one of the gentlest of the cats brought me a beautiful cedar waxwing, and she was pretty good about letting me have it. Not all of them feel that way. But, in her tussle with the bird, it appeared that she had broken one of the bird's wings. Usually I can release the birds after a while of rest and de-stressing, but this one couldn't fly away.

I had no idea how to find out if it had a broken wing, except to watch it fail at flying. I had absolutely no idea what to do with a bird that had a broken wing. Sometimes I feel guilty when I am unable to solve prob-lems in my own backyard. I expect to be able to take care of the place where I live. Well, phooey. I can't always do that.

Fortunately my community has a wildlife center with a specialist in charge of small birds. My guilt disappeared when I left the bird with the bird lady.

Today's society does have some advantages. When I fail in my expectations of doing my own income tax, I can hire a CPA. When my method of repairing the leaky faucet in the kitchen fails, I can call a plumber. We have many ways of relieving ourselves from our own expectations.

Of course, many of our expectations are unconscious. Often I don't know what I expect of myself until I fail at it. And the same for you. I become aware of my expectations when they are not met.

The doing, the doing—how hard it is to drop the idea of attainment.

Peter Matthiessen

PLAY'S THE THING

Compassion suffers miserably at the hands of competition, for compassion seeks our common likenesses—which in fact are joy and tragedy—not our differences. Yet it is competition's task to make us different—winners or losers, ins and outs.

Matthew Fox

Sometimes competition and cooperation are direct opposites. Sometimes they are very close together. "If you can't afford to lose, you can't afford to play." "Winning isn't everything, it's the only thing."

Competition gives players the opportunity to try harder, to perform better, and sometimes to learn dirty little tricks, when winning is the only thing. There are many different levels of competition. It is strange to me that all of our national sports are played and played until there is only one winner and all the rest are losers, even numero dos.

Team competition only succeeds when there is appropriate cooperation. It is impossible to move the football down the field unless the thrower throws, the receiver receives, the runner runs, and the blockers block. Although competitors don't talk much about cooperation, it is still there.

Cooperation, when it occurs, has a beauty of its own. When two of my friends and I load our tractor mower onto the truck, drive it to the place that needs mowing, mow and trim and load the trimmings, and finally come home, it brings me immense pleasure. Each of us anticipates what needs to be done next and does it. I no longer expect people to do the right thing at the right time, so when it happens, it is a joy to behold.

When I was in the seventh grade and living on the fringes of a highly conservative area of San Mateo, California, I was a pretty good athlete. We were playing softball, and my team was winning. Our side was at bat, and I'd made it to second base, when their shortstop, one of the smartest girls in the school, said something like, "Why in the world would you want to vote for Roosevelt?" She approached me belligerently with her hands on her hips. Expecting that her question had something to do with our softball game, which, of course, it did, I walked over to her, put my hands on my hips, and said something like,

"So?" She quickly moved her hand toward me and tagged me out with the ball, which was hidden under her hand. I wish I were making this up.

I knew I wasn't a real genius, but to be tricked like that in a game of fun reduced me in my own eyes to an idiot. I don't think I ever talked to her again after that. She was in a league of her own, one that was not fun.

Play is the one area in which I have excelled all my life. I don't mean professional athletics like Steve Young, Martina Hingis, or Michael Jordan perform. I mean play. There aren't too many experts in play, probably because there is no monetary gain. But the gains for the soul and spirit, and even the body, are tremendous. I have never enjoyed exercises, or jogging, or activities that have no game element.

Being an expert on play and cooperation is not like being a pro player, for whom how well you play is very serious business. Play is about fun and the thrills that come from overcoming klutziness, learning to cooperate, and sometimes even overcoming fear, as in skiing and diving. It is a great joy when, on rare occasions, you play your best, even though you may not "win" the game.

As a youngster, I played games like hide-and-go-seek, kick-the-can, racing, and roughhousing. Finally, I graduated to more adult games like tennis, badminton, swimming, and even basketball. I went from hearts and poker to bridge and crossword puzzles.

The two games that have been part of me for most of my life are bridge and badminton. After my older brothers left home, my parents and grandmother needed a fourth for bridge, so I started playing when I was around ten or twelve. They must not have expected very much, because they let me keep on playing with them. Badminton was taught at my community college, and I loved it more than anything else.

Working with others to achieve a goal can give me a feeling of accomplishment that never comes from competition, no matter how often I win. Whether in work or play, cooperation and teamwork have always been satisfying.

There are no real rules for playing, except to be as mindful and as single-minded as possible about it. I often feel myself to be the game, aware of all the players and myself together as a whole. We are not separate; we interact as our relationships change, always changing, never the same. We players are all in the present moment, never thinking about yesterday's laundry or tomorrow's ice cream cones, never expecting anything but the playing.

Interdependence is a fundamental law of nature.
Many of the smallest insects are social beings who,
without any religion, law or education survive by mutual
cooperation based on an innate recognition of their
interconnectedness.

Dalai Lama and Phil Borges

Cooperation, when it occurs, has a beauty of its own. When two of my friends and I load our tractor mower onto the truck, drive it to the place that needs mowing, mow and trim and load the trimmings, and finally come home, it brings me immense pleasure. Each of us anticipates what needs to be done next and does it. I no longer expect people to do the right thing at the right time, so when it happens, it is a joy to behold.

PART II
PERSONAL AND PROFESSONAL RELATIONSHIPS

Our personal and professional lives are fraught
with the potential for expectation. Every time we
encounter another being in a situation where there
is the possibility for a substantive and meaningful
relationship—in love and in work, for instance—there
is also the possibility for deep disappointment. It
would behoove us to be mindfully aware of both the
potential and the danger here.

SEVEN

LOVERS

The results of Karma cannot be known by thought and so should not be speculated about. Thus thinking, one would come to distraction and distress. Therefore, Ananda, do not be the judge of people; do not make assumptions about others. A person is destroyed by holding judgements about others.

From The Anguttara Nikaya

I expected people with whom I was in love to figure out what I was thinking, what I was feeling, what I was needing and wanting. Expectations of a loved one are the most difficult to realize. I have usually been so committed to my loved one that I expected the world and the universe in return. Proximity and interwoven lives lead some of us to overlook our different perspectives. I made assumptions that were incorrect and destructive. I expected others to know me better than I know me.

I became my most pitiful when these expectations failed to materialize. I did not yell or throw things. I withdrew. I fumed in terrible glaring silence. How could my partner be so inconsiderate as not to know me?

In this condition, communication is impossible. And sometimes my dark angry cloud lasted for days. Eventually, it would go away and we would go on as before—still not having communicated. So, of course, the cycle continued.

I am not a psychic person. How could I expect my partner to be psychic?

I have since learned that communication is the most difficult thing to achieve in a partnership, for everyone, not just for me, and that communication is necessary, no matter how embarrassing or painful. Differences must be appreciated and allowed.

Today, more and more couples are attending group counseling to find out about their own expectations and their partners' expectations, so they won't get into so many problems. Many people don't know what their own values, preferences, and beliefs are until they meet a partner who affirms or challenges them, and some not until they get some kind of instruction or engage in open discussion. Before marriage many people don't know how hard it is to live with another person. Fortunately, in college, I had a few roommates. That helped, but living with anyone is tough—a good thing to know ahead of time.

Knowing beforehand how each other feels about money, play, cooperation, goals, and other people is important in keeping expectations realistic and at a minimum. When we don't expect the world, compassion is much easier.

Perhaps my love has been imperfect. Thich Nhat Hanh says that if you don't understand the one you love, it is not true love. I must be very mindful and look deeply in order to see and understand the needs and goals and sufferings of the one I love.

We are all interconnected and constantly changing and flowing, not always in predictable directions. Paying attention and living right now, here, is what it is all about. If we don't find our happiness here, now, where will we find it? Tomorrow is another bunch of heres and nows that we must learn to live in as each occurs. Otherwise, we will miss the whole world.

Right now I'm working on loving with understanding, but without expecting anything in return. I may need another lifetime or two.

Compassion is everywhere. Compassion is the world's richest energy source. Now that the world is a global village we need compassion more than ever . . . not for altruism's sake, nor philosophy's sake, or theology's sake, but for survival's sake.

Matthew Fox

E I G H T

PARENTING

*In our increasingly touch-deprived society, much of our
time is taken up in disembodied, non-interactive activities. As a culture, less and less are we together with others, talking, playing music, singing, dancing, fishing or
playing basketball, cards or chess, cooking and eating
together. Hugging, snuggling, holding hands, being
together in silence, watching logs burning in the fire
place, looking at the stars, listening and being listened
to, gazing at our loved ones, are all in danger of being
lost to us.*

Myla and Jon Kabat-Zinn

Beginning parents are beginners, even the ones who take
courses, read books, and have had younger siblings to

practice on. You need a license to drive a car, but you don't need a license to be a parent. Although parenting is probably the one most important thing a man or woman can do during a lifetime, our culture makes no effort to prepare us for this immense project.

Good parents somehow learn to keep their expectations to a minimum and their appreciation to a maximum. There are so many things we can enjoy about our children without making judgments about them. But many of us tend to want our children to change and become better, no matter how good they already are.

Our own examples of mindfulness, compassion, and patience can help our children learn from our presence how to live their own lives. And when we share with them our way of dealing with expectations, we give them room to consider dealing with their own expectations. When they know how we struggle to do what is good and beautiful and true, they will begin to learn mindfulness. When they see how difficult it is to keep from putting expectations on someone else, they will begin to expect less of others.

The way we see others and govern our behavior can occur without our being aware of what our expectations are doing to us. If we can be as mindful as possible when we create these expectations, we will be less apt to cause suffering and frustration in our children. Our children have much to teach us if we will mindfully pay attention.

I probably had the best mother in the world. When I got interested in something, she helped me pursue it.

When I failed at something, she helped me change gears and either improve or find other interests. Her love and acceptance were constant, her expectations minimal.

While in our community college, I learned to drink and thought that being a bartender would be great because I loved to listen to people's stories. Mom was ready to finance bartender school when I discovered that I could play for the rest of my life if I became a PE teacher. So she financed college. Having a mother like this has made many things possible for me that would not have happened if I had been put in a box of someone else's expectations.

But many of us don't let on that we don't know what we're doing. The less we know what we're doing, the more we do it with authority and the more closed we are to learning what is actually out there.

Our children are not us. Though they may have some of our DNA and may have resided in one of us for nine months, they have a new home now as well as other DNA mixed in with ours. That makes them separate but equal. And when they're small, that makes us even more responsible for doing the right thing. But what is the right thing? Even Dr. Spock didn't have simple answers. If we listen, our children can teach us.

We were all beginners once in everything we have done. In parenting, we're a beginner every day, moment to moment, because we change and our children change, moment to moment. The old tricks no longer work. Expecting our children to be better than they are doesn't work. If we can live in the here and now, be a part of parenting as it is happening, we will make fewer mistakes.

The pressure of parenting is enormous. The pressure of being a child is enormous.

If we can just realize these things and take them into consideration when we start making our expectations list, we may minimize frustration and suffering and maximize happiness and growth in all parties concerned.

Perhaps the greatest social service that can be rendered by anyone to the country and to mankind is to bring up a family.

George Bernard Shaw

The way we see others and govern our behavior can occur without our being aware of what our expectations are doing to us. If we can be as mindful as possible when we create these expectations, we will be less apt to cause suffering and frustration in our children. Our children have much to teach us if we will mindfully pay attention.

NINE

FRIENDS

There was a sign in a casino in Las Vegas that a friend of mine took and now has in his therapy room; it says, "You must be present to win." It's true in Las Vegas, and it's true in therapy, and it's true in tennis, and it's the starting point in meditation.

Jack Kornfield

Friends add a lot of spice to life. I don't expect this, it just happens. I've been fortunate to have had many friends over the years. There are several old friends that I still keep in touch with. Maybe only once a year, but that is enough.

In the old days, I had friends who should have known what I expected of them even if I didn't tell them. I had friends who let me down; that is, they did not live up to my expectations. That was my fault. Their expectations just didn't match my expectations—and at that time I did have expectations.

Some friends were more difficult to be with because of their expectations of me. Some were more needy, less secure, wanted more and more of me. I've had two friends whom I asked to leave my life because I couldn't keep giving what they didn't really need. This was quite difficult because they didn't understand, nor were they ready to listen to what they didn't want to hear. I am not proud of this. I was just inadequate.

I don't think I pick my friends, just as I don't think I pick my lovers. They just happen. Sometimes it's things we have in common. Sometimes it's our unusual differences and utter surprise and joy at discovering what we never would have expected of each other. One friend in particular loves to play on my naivete, shocking me as often as she can with the real world where she lives. I love her for that.

For me, being a friend means appreciating everything, being helpful, having ideas about where to go for answers, and doing fun things together. Like the animals that live with me, each friend brings me joy—in different ways with each friend—but joy. I just hope I bring joy in return. I am still learning to be a good friend.

Friends can be strong or fragile, wild or serene. They come in all shapes and continue to test my mindfulness and challenge my expectations. The seeds of friendship are not different from the seeds of love. Mindfulness and being present can only help. Eliminating expectations and just enjoying whatever happens helps make my friends surprising and exciting. And as we develop our love of ourselves, we will be able to love others more completely.

The secret of the mountains is that the mountains simply exist, as I do myself: the mountains exist simply, which I do not. The mountains have no "meaning," they ARE meaning; the mountains are.

Peter Matthiessen

TEN

NEIGHBORS

The truth you believe in and cling to makes you unavailable to hear anything new.

Pema Chodron

Like marriage or partnerships, neighborship requires meeting the expectations of those around you. And each neighborhood is different.

People engage in a complicated dance, a dance with rules that are neither stated nor written down. In crowded neighborhoods, where you park your car, where you put your garbage can, and how late you play music have rules. In more rural neighborhoods, there are rules to pick the right burn day to burn your leaves.

Upon moving into a new neighborhood, you must learn a new dance, sometimes with very intricate steps. Of course, not all neighbors bother with the dance. Either they aren't aware of it, or they prefer to ignore it. The dancing neighbors learn to adjust, or sometimes they seek revenge.

Mindfulness seems to work with neighbors as well as with cats and goats. So far, I've enjoyed my neighbors very much, and they don't seem to be annoyed with me. I have one conservative neighbor on each side of me and a wetlands area for my backyard. I tend to be liberal, though it depends. Both neighbors love to bait me into taking some political stance, from green environment, to loggers' rights, to all the governmental red tape, to taxes. Mostly I listen. I do not expect them to agree with me. I try to listen to their views and see what I can learn. They think they have won a victory when I agree with them, while I know deep down they're just happy to share their views. Once in a while, they even listen to me. In this instance, I'm pretty good at not expecting. So we dance on, while each maintains individual integrity.

Being in the present moment makes things go in slow motion. I can actually see and hear and feel what others are saying and doing. We cannot change other people's opinions, although if we are mindful, we can let them know of some things that are possible.

The Buddha said: "To be attached to a certain view and to look down upon other views as inferior . . . this the wise call a fetter."

From The Sutta Nipata

Being in the present moment makes things go in slow motion. I can actually see and hear and feel what others are saying and doing. We cannot change other people's opinions, although if we are mindful, we can let them know of some things that are possible.

ELEVEN

PRIVATE ENTERPRISE

Only human beings love profit and fame. Profit is constant grasping, not only for the material world, but for a psychological and a spiritual life as well. It's pretty busy. Even though this grasping is for the spiritual world, there is still craving.

Dainin Katagiri

One giddy summer afternoon when the sun was bright and the sky was blue, a friend and I were enjoying the planet at a beautiful mountain lake. The lake had three tourist towns around it and lots of boating and swimming activities. We both thought it would be wonderful if we could afford to spend more time there and started thinking about ways to make it possible. We were both teachers at different universities, with summers off—technically at least—and fairly low salaries.

My friend had a brother-in-law who ran a gift and garden shop in her hometown, and we tended to think that might be a good choice of business for the lake area. We also had two friends who had been laid off and needed jobs. Although we fed lots of data into our mental computers, those two items seemed to be the salient points.

We decided to start a gift and garden shop in which we could work during the busy summers and our two friends could work year-round. What a great idea! We even expected to make money and perhaps retire to the shop and the lake when the time came.

We bought an inexpensive house on the main street and turned it into a store. Our friends trained with the brother-in-law in how to run a gift and garden shop. We all went to the annual Gift Show in San Francisco and ordered all kinds of wonderful things that we were sure people would want to buy.

We decided on a name and a logo and a sign for out front and finally opened that fall. Tourist season was over—but it was a quiet time when we could learn the process without too many customers. The store had living quarters in the back, which, though tight, could accommodate all four of us.

We expected the locals to be delighted with our obvious love of their town and their lake. We thought they would welcome our commitment and energy and flock to support our endeavors.

No one came to welcome us. No one offered even one word of optimism about our project. They probably thought we were invaders who wanted to take away something from their beautiful lake. They may have been reluctant to let outsiders in or to allow anything that might cause a growth in population.

This was our first inkling of reality. We did have two or three customers a day, mostly from out of town. But, heck, this was only our first year. Things would pick up.

Spending most weekends at the lake was difficult for my new partner and me because we were both quite serious about our teaching. We came from opposite directions to get to the lake, so we couldn't even help each other with the driving.

We succeeded in operating that first year. Then, unfortunately, our two friends found new jobs more in keeping with their fields and had to leave the shop. But summer was almost over, and the two of us could handle it. And we did.

In the fall, we hired a local woman to clerk for us Monday through Friday, but one of us had to be there every weekend to restock, keep the books, clean the place, and whatever.

We managed to last the three years that IRS allows a small business to lose money before they declare it a hobby. Yes, we lost money every year, even though neither of us received a salary or expenses. Fortunately, when we sold the store, real estate values had gone up enough so that we made a little back on our building and didn't feel like total failures.

My partner and I both needed much recovery time. We rarely saw each other and rarely went to the lake after that. I felt as if I had lost a very dear friend as well as a home. My thoughts of becoming a member of this lovely community were dashed. It was a closed community where they chose who would enter. I guess they were more committed to blocking out invaders than we were to breaking down their resistance.

Such noble expectations! So much energy! So many risks! Especially when we could have just enjoyed the lake without invading it.

I've been much more mindful since this experience. We did not walk in anyone's footprints. We did not learn their dance. We were not there when we needed to be. Our expectations and theirs never got together.

We don't have to like a rainy day, or a wet, cold, slushy December afternoon, necessarily, we just have to take it, and pass through it, without dwelling on our preference that it be different. We don't have to wait for the sun to come out, either, before we can be happy.

We can be happy every day.

D. W. Moore

*Such noble expectations! So much energy!
So many risks! Especially when we could have
just enjoyed the lake without invading it.*

TWELVE

GOVERNMENT WORK

Usually, we don't undertake anything without having expectations about what it will be like, what it will do for us, what its value will be. Our expectations often get us where we need to be; but they also can seriously impede our ability to experience anything freshly because we insist on measuring it against those expectations. They create the most problems when we hold them rigidly and when they are unexamined or unconscious.

Myla and Jon Kabat-Zinn

My oldest brother, Bill, spent much of World War II in Italy and learned to speak Italian and German. After the war, he returned to Europe on the GI Bill, studying at the University of Heidelberg, the University of Zurich, and the

University of Florence. He spent three years over there and loved it all. Often, the GI Bill allowed him to live in palaces—drafty old palaces, but palaces, nonetheless.

I was enthralled with the idea of going to Europe, but I knew I could never afford the cost of getting there. So I decided to get a job that would take me there. Having taught for two years in high school and two years in college, I found myself qualified to be a recreation director in a service club in Laon, France, working as a civilian for the government. A service club is a recreational facility designed to entertain the troops, much as the USO did. Our service club was on an air force base, and I was housed in the bachelor officers' quarters along with other civilians as well as officers.

The thought of working for the government was intriguing. I had thought of the government as an entity that was there to help the people. Why else would it exist? Not only to help the people, but to keep the cost down for those of us who paid taxes. I abruptly learned that my expectations were not always correct, and I learned how naive I was about the real world.

Apart from Ping-Pong and pool tournaments, arts and crafts instruction, provision of musical instruments and instruction, visits from Hollywood notables, dances with local French girls, and TV films, we arranged tours to any place where we could get enough people interested in going. I saw much of France, Germany, Austria, Belgium, Holland, and England—and I was paid for it!

During my second year there, we built a new service club, so I was in on the planning, architecture, construction, and decoration. It was a sad awakening when I saw members of our government buying all kinds of unnecessary things that they thought would be cute, or that they thought they would be able to take home with them when they left. Many of the projects had to be redone over and over again because of incompetence in workmanship. At the least, I had expected the members of our government to be efficient, effective, and functional. Most of my expectations had been built on some kind of wishful thinking, not on reality.

The base librarian was my "drain mate"—we shared the bathroom between our two bedrooms. She was always saying, "When I go home, I'm going to write my congressman." But, like most of us working for the government, she was not about to upset the gravy train while she was on it. I never did write my congressman, but I'm sure my drain mate did.

She was a real critic. She kept track of all the overages and underages—the $700 toilet seats and the $600 hammers. She knew what she was talking about and expected the government to eliminate such waste. I didn't have the conviction she had.

I did learn to listen more carefully and to realize that throughout history there have been those who will use others for their own gain. I became aware of the fact that I was using the government. I took this job to see Europe, and I did see Europe. The government didn't let me down.

And so, my fellow Americans, ask not what your country can do for you, ask what you can do for your country.
John Fitzgerald Kennedy

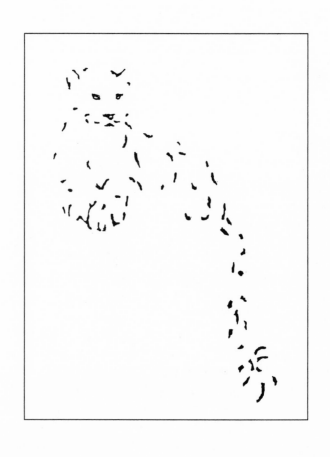

THIRTEEN

TEACHING

The way we look at the world informs us about what it is and who we are. The way we treat our knowledge leads us to a certain picture of the world. This triple relationship between mind, knowledge and the world has to be thought through again.

Henryk Skolinowski

I have been a teacher for over forty years—more time than I have spent being anything else, except human and female.

Teaching is a mysterious profession. All teachers, being people, are different. All teaching is different. Each day is an experiment—sometimes quite boring to students and teacher alike, sometimes quite wonderful.

Teaching students is certainly rife with expectations, because it has the potential for exerting a strong influence on so many people. And I was teaching future teachers, so the potential to spread the good word was exponentially greater.

We keep thinking we can teach teachers how to teach. I love the new saying: "Those who can, do; those who can't, teach; those who can't teach, teach teachers to teach." I guess it's OK to joke about myself, but what I'm leading up to is that one of the tenets of teaching is to motivate. And one of the big tools of motivation is expectation. Expect each student to produce. Expect each student to retain your every word and teaching process and become even more learned than you are.

I did experiential things so that students would grasp more than words. My students played games that showed the difference between cooperation and competition. My students tried to figure out the basic elements of each other's teaching methods, philosophies, and beliefs as they participated in mini-teaching projects.

We did student-centered teaching, group interaction teaching, self-graded teaching, contract teaching. I even tried content lecturing—the so-called traditional method. But we all lecture differently, and we all value different content. So how do we measure results?

I wanted my students to know how their teaching would affect their students—when I didn't even know how my teaching affected my students.

Earlier, my tests were ferocious. I expected my students to learn everything. But just because I tested everything, this did not mean that students learned everything or even that I taught everything. Somewhere along the way I started expecting that students might learn 50 percent of the course material, and then I expected even less. Finally, my tests consisted of only about fifteen study questions handed out in advance—of course, they were broad questions such as "compare and contrast . . ." or "describe the process of . . . ," covering maybe 20 percent of the course (but the most important 20 percent, from my point of view).

I was a rabid teacher. I turned down dates, opportunities to go to the opera, the ballet, the movies, because I had to spend my time being a better teacher. I had a great deal to learn. It takes at least one hundred hours to prepare a one-hour lecture—getting a basic foundation, reading all the latest research, comparing old with new, debating with colleagues, getting expert opinions, and putting it all together in some form that makes sense, at least to me. And then the same lecture has to be updated next time, because everything changes—sometimes a lot. Creating new and different courses always seemed to take me at least a year. One new course preparation I managed to accomplish on a sabbatical leave. Two others I did during leaves without pay. Yes, I was a very rabid teacher.

Originally, I thought that because I was a good person, I would be a good teacher. Forget that. Good personhood is not necessarily good teaching. And, originally, I expected to be all things to all people. Well, that didn't last long, but it was somewhat devastating when I realized that it wasn't possible.

Once I figured out that I couldn't be a perfect teacher even if I stayed awake and worked at it twenty-four hours a day, I began to lighten up. I probably became a better teacher then, because the expectations began to disappear. Encouraging and appreciating students is different from expecting things of students.

To know and to be unknowing is best;
Not to know and to be knowing is sickness,
Only by being sick of our sickness
Are we not sick,
He's sick of his sickness
And therefore is not sick.

Herryman Mauer

Originally, I thought that because I was a good person, I would be a good teacher. Forget that. Good personhood is not necessarily good teaching. And, originally, I expected to be all things to all people. Well, that didn't last long, but it was somewhat devastating when I realized that it wasn't possible.

FOURTEEN

FAIRNESS AND JUSTICE

The best answer to injustice is not justice, but compassion or love.

Charlotte Joko Beck

I once believed in fairness and justice. Expected fairness and justice.

When I was little, I had to learn to take turns and to share. I had to learn to be fair. It did not come naturally. I was the youngest in a family with two older brothers who simply would not put up with me when I was not fair. They would not tolerate a self-centered, egotistical little sister. By the time I was grown, I had learned fairness well and expected fairness wherever I went.

There are times when I wonder which planet I came from. But I must have been thirty or forty before I realized that fairness and justice are just words—human concepts—ideals that seem nice: expectations. I began to see that there isn't a Fairness God who just sits around and evens things out.

At first, when bad things happened to me, I thought life and the world weren't fair, and, of course, I got angry. But as I began to grow up and take a better look at the world, I began to realize how fortunate I was.

Good things happened to me that didn't necessarily happen to others, and I wondered about fairness. I didn't have to worry about my next meal, or cholera, or racial wars. Because my parents were educated and wise, I became educated, but not wise yet, and didn't have to worry about getting a job or being unable to read my driving test or program my VCR. In the city where I've chosen to live, I don't have to worry about crime or traffic snarls or too many confining rules and regulations.

Now I know that compassion is more realistic than fairness. Though fairness is a nice ideal, it is not something I worry about or get angry about anymore. That's not what is important.

This doesn't mean that I don't still strive to be fair in my dealings with people. I just don't expect to get fairness, and when I do, it's great.

But what is fairness? When raising children, you can't treat each child equally because they don't come in the same shape or size or with the same desires or wants or needs. Jim may need a bike, but Alice is barely able to operate her trike. Being mindful makes me more fair about differences. There's not a lot of fairness because free-willed human beings aren't always responsible for their actions. Not all of us are mindful of the consequences.

There is always inequity in life. Some men are killed in a war and some men are wounded, and some men never leave the country. . . . Life is unfair.

John Fitzgerald Kennedy

PART III
CULTURAL EXPECTATIONS

In America, we have a long history of expectations about what being an American means. Some of these ideals are heroism, individualism, ambition, independence. But our society also puts expectations on us that are detrimental to our own identity and individuality. It seems useful to point out the cultural expectations that too often harm us. Some of them have certainly harmed me, and my new awareness of them has helped me keep them at bay.

FIFTEEN

STEREOTYPES

Who would question that culture represents the highest achievement of life? Or that our civilization as practiced by us is not the "great goal of evolution"? We have been conditioned to believe this implicitly. We presume that without culture man would be only another animal, a creature of darkness without meaning or purpose.

Joseph Pearce

Stereotyping can be a good thing. It can tell you if that's a lion or a gazelle that's chasing you, so you can know if you should run faster. But it won't tell you if this particular lion has a thorn in its foot and needs help, if it's pretty old and has lost all its teeth, or if it has just eaten a big meal. If God is in the details, stereotyping is ungodly.

Nowadays, when we're no longer in the jungle, stereotyping is usually a hindrance. "Young white male" does not always mean arrogance and destructiveness, any more than "old black female" means obeisance and docility. Instead of being surrounded by lions we're surrounded by cultural stereotypes (behaviorial expectations) that have a great bearing on the way we look at ourselves and each other.

The two following rather broad stereotypes are just some examples of this problem.

FEMININITY

We are all suffering from the ravages of our cultural expectations—women no less than men—but with many different twists and turns. Women are not valued as highly as men in our culture. In some other times and places, many female babies were eliminated at birth, so in comparison, perhaps we are lucky to be in this country today. Still, we do learn to devalue our womanhood and alienate ourselves from ourselves and other women. Women are expected to be sexual objects in our culture, so we spend much money and time and do many weird things to play that role.

Is anatomy destiny? Is physiognomy character? Research shows that attractive people get more respect and admiration and are believed to be smarter, kinder, and more loving than the rest of us. If anatomy is destiny, if good looks create character, then morality must be the creation of plastic surgery, diet and exercise regimes, fashion

designers, and the cosmetics industry. But human knowledge and character do not arise out of hair color, height,
or weight, nor do they arise out of skin color or gender.
They arise out of being human and from the way each of
us deals with the joys and suffering that go along with
being human.

Impossible expectations of what is beautiful and
acceptable cause women to squeeze their feet into tiny
spiked shoes, scrunch into push-up bras, pierce, bleach,
wax, and pluck. I've done all these things for more years
than I care to remember. Now breast implants, lip
enhancements, liposuction, and buttock lifts are common.

When I was growing up, I knew I didn't look quite
right. Although I had dates, they weren't with the boys I
wanted to be with. Losing weight was always the first
thing I would work on in my attempts to become a more
dateable person. Then clothing, but having the right
clothes cost a lot of money, which I didn't have. Then
makeup. I was such a klutz with makeup. I'm sure now
that I looked much better without any at all. It never
occurred to me to work on being a better person.

I am finally learning that positive self-esteem is more
directly related to maturity, creativity, confidence, and
responsibility. Conforming to society's expectations for
appearance is really not important compared to the contributions we can make to life on this planet. What we do
is so much more important than how we look.

When appearance is much more important than
achievement, by cultural standards, something is dreadful-

ly wrong with that culture. Self-modification always seems necessary, and our bodies are never good enough in this no-win game. We keep doing more and more to become something we are not. Our facades and false appearances only demoralize us and reduce our self-esteem. When love and acceptance are based on beauty, some of us who are not beautiful give what we would not otherwise give to achieve acceptance. Playing the only game in town will only lead us deeper and deeper into the pit of consumerism.

Until recently, women didn't compete with men. We competed for men. Women also were not known for their efficient administrative abilities, yet we were efficient executives in running our own homes. Fear of failure rested with the men around us, our husbands, sons, fathers. We were expected to have good men around, however.

My two brothers were expected to get good grades, go on to college, and become something good. Although I was expected to go to college, it didn't really matter if I became anything at all. What beautiful freedom I had, and I didn't even realize it. Competition in the work world didn't really exist for me . . . probably because if I failed, I could just get married.

Now with women in the workforce, all this is changing. Today, women are burdened with many of the expectations that used to be reserved for men. This may not be a good thing. We always seem to be catching up with the male point of view. Sometime we need to let them catch up with ours.

We are what we do and feel. We don't need mirrors to be successful human beings. Yet we have been taught to follow rules that society thinks are more important than our own individual selves. Instead of accepting these cultural expectations, we could be creating a world of our own.

I had to live through the first feminist movement to realize that something was wrong with our culture. Until then, I just believed that's the way things were. I accepted my role without question.

Even a year or two into the feminist movement, I still didn't get it—until one day early in the semester when I was working on learning the names of all my students. I realized that I knew all the men's names; it was the women's names I was still working on. Even I didn't value women as much as men.

Women have much to offer the world in their patience, love, compassion, and appreciation. Women obviously commit fewer aggressive acts than men, crimes of all sorts, wars of all sorts. We can enhance our role by emphasizing our appreciation and encouragement of others, not just our children, but each other and ourselves.

MASCULINITY

I don't know about being a man firsthand, but there have been enough men in my life for me to be aware of some things. And I thought being a woman was difficult! Competition and fear of failure seem to dominate the male identity. Being the opposite of the mother is instilled early, along with fear of intimacy and emotions, fear of weakness, and fear of aging with its loss of hero status and job identity. Manhood is a perpetual struggle that is never finally and forever won.

Men are in the same vicelike grip of cultural expectations as are women. Men can be beautiful, sensitive, constructive, tenderhearted, nurturing, and miraculous creatures. They have the opportunity to be teachers, mentors, and colleagues in helping others to be successful in a world filled with ambiguous dangers. There is healing power in fathering and manhood and responsibility for the new generation. Men could be mentors for other men and boys, but so many choose to compete instead.

Fortunately, most of the men I know are disgusted with the macho risks imposed on them by society. They are beginning to rebel against society's expectations.

One of the strongest men I know is Tom, a building contractor, who is in the process of building my garage. He also added two bedrooms and a bath to my home a few years ago. He is an excellent, though not extravagant, carpenter. He has a daughter, Lily, who is three years old, and since his divorce he spends Mondays and Tuesdays just being with her, doing things with her like playing games, learning about flowers and birds and animals together, going to Marine World. This choice has reduced his income, but not his enjoyment and commitment to life. He is always thoughtful and has constructive ideas for accomplishing my goals in more elegant, and often less expensive, ways. He already is mindful of the present moment, as well as patient, compassionate, and loving with all around him.

During hot wars and cold wars, our country has deliberately developed the masculine ideal believed necessary to protect our nation. When these wars are over, it takes decades to dismantle the masculine and feminine roles that have been so well instilled. The role of women as vulnerable and the role of men as protectors were important in creating men who could in fact protect us and die for their country. The more vulnerable the women, the more protective the men. The fear of not being man enough is linked to repression of women and homophobia, involving the fear of being weak or feminine. The stereotype of what men are expected to be is just that: expectations put on our men by our culture.

In the meantime more and more men are becoming the targets of all the beauty industries: hairstyling, fashion, cosmetic surgery, hair coloring and replacement, health and fitness, height enhancement, weight control, penile implants, sexual technique videos, video dating, computer coupling, and virtual reality sex.

There is considerable evidence that indicates that men can be nonviolent regardless of testosterone levels, provided that they learn and value nonviolence. But our culture expects men to be violent and aggressive and to commit or defeat evil. Men are beginning to see themselves as puppets playing a masculine role with no separate identity . . . as sex machines as well as fighting machines.

Today, more and more men compete in financial ways; they don't fight physically anymore, they just make more money and often flaunt it.

Men have met the enemy and it is masculinity, a culturally created trap. Both men and women are caught in this trap of imitating the same-sex parental stereotype, perpetuating the problems of their parents instead of writing a future that belongs to themselves. Science and technology have made sex roles unnecessary. Our ability to adapt and learn is our most important asset now. Men's involvement in child care and nurturing is crucial to bringing men into their rightful place of giving life instead of taking life. We can create our own evolution by the rearing and loving of children by both men and women.

The reason we're often not there for others . . . whether for our child or our mother or someone who is insulting us or someone who frightens us . . . is that we're not there for ourselves.

Pema Chodron

I am finally learning that positive self-esteem is more directly related to maturity, creativity, confidence, and responsibility. Conforming to society's expectations for appearance is really not important compared to the contributions we can make to life on this planet. What we do is so much more important than how we look.

SIXTEEN

THE FACADE OF BODIES

When you give up your ego you gain the whole process and pattern of life. You gain your life and the whole of life.

Thich Nhat Hanh

When I was sixteen, I was 5'8" in height and weighed 135 pounds. But Ingrid Bergman, about the same height, weighed 128 pounds. Since she was my main cultural role model, I went on my first diet, expecting that I would then be just like her. I did manage to lose about three pounds during that first diet. I had bought into my own expectations and wanted to look like the images on the screen. I dieted for years and years after that, always gaining more and more weight over those years.

It's kind of sad to note that every time I gained some weight I would think I looked awful. Then, after I'd gained even more weight, I'd think back to the previous weight gain and wish I could be that much smaller. I never was happy with my weight once the dieting entered my life.

We often expect ourselves to be perfect, and appearance is just one of the most important ways we try to show this perfection. We create a lot of suffering for ourselves, struggling with all kinds of societal expectations that we accept as appropriate for ourselves. Size and shape are just two of them.

Perfecting the self is not an unworthy idea, but size and shape are minor accomplishments compared to perfecting kindness and compassion and other more lasting qualities.

We don't have to accept this societal notion of thinness. We are the ones in control of whether this is a good notion or a bad notion, in our own lives, at least. Most of us accept the absurd idea that looking like a movie star is good. Yet each one of us creates our own range of perfection, and each one of us can change it.

Are society's expectations correct? Were they correct when women wore corsets and bustles and fainted a lot? Were they correct when we were skinny flappers in the twenties or more buxom women à la Marilyn Monroe in the 1950s? Are they correct now? Are they ever correct?

Buddha said that suffering is caused by attachment to desire. The more we desire, cling, and grasp, the more suffering we feel when these desires are not satisfied, when our expectations are not fulfilled, when our ego controls our expectations.

Seeing the reality of the situation helps us remove desire, habit, judgment, and expectation. Must we always feel guilty when we eat or angry when society parades another skinny role model in front of us? We can choose our reactions and our expectations if we are mindful.

Between the ages of thirty-five and forty, when I had a few gray hairs growing into my hairline and was tired of plucking them out, I became a bleached blond. At the same time, I also bought contact lenses and wore them, even though they never felt comfortable. And along with this, I went to the fat doctor. He gave me 20–30 pills to take each day, and they always made me feel lousy. But what's a little lousiness if one can be thin? I did lose 15–20 pounds and kept it off for a few years.

About five years later, I looked in the mirror and wondered what color my hair really was. I also longed to get rid of my contact lenses and feel a little bit more comfortable again. Comfort? What was I thinking of? If you want comfort, Kid, give up the fat doctor. So I gave them all up. I was tired of feeling lousy. I became me again. Although I wasn't Ingrid Bergman, I was me again.

Was Ingrid Bergman happy? Was she comfortable with her life? She probably had more internal and external expectations to deal with than I would ever have imagined.

Freedom from thinking about and being obsessed with food is a more potent force in losing weight than dieting could ever be. Will we be attractive when we lose ten pounds? Twenty pounds? When do we suddenly become attractive? Are thinner people happier? I'm beginning to think happiness is liking ourselves and being proud of what we are.

The diet and fitness industries are dependent on the beliefs that 1) being fat is somehow immoral, and 2) fat people must have no willpower. We now know that when we diet, our bodies protect us from famine by reducing our metabolic rate, increasing our appetite, utilizing food more efficiently, and reducing our activity levels. So when we diet, we tend to gain weight. Dieting also makes us obsess about food. We can stop feeling guilty and constantly thinking about food. Part of mindfulness is sometimes not to think about food (or cigarettes or whatever) and to think about something else instead. When I can think mindfully instead of ravenously, I can eliminate the obsession.

So I don't diet anymore. I am overweight, but that's not important. When I do eat, I eat things I really love. Eating has become delightful instead of guilt-ridden. I no longer have any expectations of getting thinner or fatter.

Somehow I had the expectation that changing the outside would change the inside. Perhaps I didn't give others enough credit for being able to see the real me. I thought they would just see the surface, the facade, so I had to be sure that that surface was good enough to gain their approval. Kindness and compassion do not come from body sizes or clothing styles. They come from patience and love and empathy. These are attitudes we can develop and change.

I have learned to have love and compassion for myself as I am. I no longer have to buy into the cultural neurosis, but this has taken me many, many years. I hope you don't wait so long.

Changes in attitudes never come easily. The development of love and compassion is a wide round curve that can be negotiated only slowly, not a sharp corner that can be turned all at once. It comes with daily practice.

Dalai Lama and Phil Borges

SEVENTEEN

CONSUMERISM

We are what we think.
All that we are arises with our thoughts.
With our thoughts we make the world.
Speak or act with an impure mind
And trouble will follow you
As the wheel follows the ox that draws the cart.

We are what we think.
All that we are arises with our thoughts.
With our thoughts we make the world.
Speak or act with a pure mind
And happiness will follow you
As your shadow, unshakable.

How can a troubled mind
Understand the way?
Your worst enemy cannot harm you
As much as your thoughts, unguarded.
But once mastered,
No one can help you as much,
Not even your father or your mother.

From The Dhammapada

A lot of our expectations are prepackaged for us by those with influence over us: parents, church, media, teachers, and so on. And we tend to expect that these authorities are correct.

As have most cultures in the past, our culture produces all kinds of problems with stereotyping, role expectations, limitations on what is beautiful, and all kinds of unconscious demands on our behavior. The miracles that make up each one of us are called into question thousands of times each day by those seeking to make money from our insecurities. Our miracles are belittled and brought under thought control. We tend to overlook the financial realities of consumerism and become something other than what we want to be. We may never even find out what we want to be. The cosmetics industry, the fashion industry, the medical industry, the diet industry, the fitness industry, the tobacco industry, and the advertising and propaganda industries all make enormous amounts of money by toying with impossible expectations.

Expectations can affect our health. Studies of the placebo response indicate that if you expect a particular medicine to help you, it will, even if in reality it is just a sugar pill. Studies of teachers and students have shown that when the teachers were led to believe that some normal students had high IQs, the students performed better because the teachers expected better performance. When students were labeled dull, they turned out dull because of teacher expectations. There are many more studies that show similar effects of expectation.

Scientists operate on the basis of expectation. They study things that fit their expectations. If there were no expectations about an area of knowledge, it would not be studied.

I smoked for thirty years, starting when I was eighteen. I wanted to be an adult, and images of adults showed them smoking. My parents smoked. My friends smoked. All the movie stars smoked. So I smoked, and I became an adult! I think it was smoking that gave me headaches. I'm sure it cut down on my endurance when I played badminton. The expectation that smoking makes the adult is ridiculous.

When I was about forty-five, I started on a path of giving up smoking. I tried quitting on my own, expecting that I could quit by sheer will, and that lasted about a month. I tried hypnosis, and that lasted about a month. I tried electric shock, and that lasted about a month. With everything I tried, I seemed to be able to grit my teeth and hold my breath for about a month, and then everything went plooey. I had given my will away to the tobacco industry. By the time I was forty-eight, I was finally ready to quit and just did it. After all, I was finally an adult.

Changing the outside is supposed to change the inside. We think that by remodeling ourselves every day into something we are not, we will become loved or rich or employed or famous. Our identities are wrapped up in the need to be beautiful or powerful or successful or happy or sexy through the use of consumer products. Appearances, cars, houses, slim bodies, perfect faces, have become more important than identity, substance, and reality. As we "progress" into the future of consumerism, we are achieving objectification for all, not just women and children. We are known by what we buy, not by what we do.

We do not have to approve of or collude with a culture that condemns us. We not only expect ourselves to become good, beautiful, and enlightened when we collude with our culture, but we expect others to join with us in being as phony as we are and in behaving like puppets controlled by consumer industries. Perhaps if we could learn to minimize our own expectations of ourselves, consumer industries would learn to minimize their expectations of us, too.

We can all be empowered by choosing what we really want for ourselves, not what would fit in with all these outside expectations. We can all be empowered by appreciating each other as we are, without the false appearances and false hopes. Cats and goats don't think about appearance to determine their value. As our culture dictates what our bodies should be, we are allowing our culture to take charge of our minds, spirits, and expectations of ourselves.

Mindfulness can help us avoid falling into the pit. If we pay attention in each moment, we will know what will work for us.

On the other hand, you could just relax and realize that, behind all the worry, complaint, and disapproval that goes on in your mind, the sun is always coming up in the morning, moving across the sky and going down in the evening. The birds are always out there collecting their food and making their nests and flying across the sky. The grass is always being blown by the wind or standing still. Food and flowers and trees are growing out of the earth. There's enormous richness. You could develop your passion for life and your curiosity and your interest. You could connect with your joyfulness. You could start right now.

Pema Chodron

EIGHTEEN

RETIRING INTO LIFE

*We don't have to get rid of all our neurotic tendencies;
what we do is begin to see how funny they are, and then
they're just part of fun and life, the fun of living with
other people. They're all crazy. And so are we, of course.
But we never really see that we're crazy; that's our pride.
Of course I'm not crazy . . . after all I'm the teacher.*

Charlotte Joko Beck

I'm now a senior citizen and expected to behave as such.
Mostly, as a senior, I'm expected to be invisible, which is
easy to do. It is also liberating. I don't have to buy into any
of our consumer culture's expectations that we should all
look young and never grow old. Some of my friends buy

into this expectation, and they look very good for their age; if that's what they want, I'm happy for them.

All seniors, myself included, worry about deteriorating and becoming helpless and a burden on family and friends. But most research shows that if you use your brain, you won't lose your brain. If you use your body, you won't lose your body.

The brain and body will actually shrink if not active. We are just learning some of the miracles that prolong life and increase intellectual capacity. The miracles involve seeking new challenges, learning more and more different kinds of activities, and thereby increasing the quantity and quality of brain tissue. The more education you have, the more learning opportunities you pursue, the more actively you are involved in redesigning and cultivating your activities, the longer you will live and the longer you will continue to think.

I've retired and live on one acre with my nephew, five cats, and three pygmy goats. I'm trying to learn to write fiction in nonacademic, nonscholarly ways, a task that is harder than I expected it would be. I've had a chance to try a new career, one that I never imagined I might want until I reached the age of fifty. I wish I'd planned for growing old and the possibility that I might want to write fiction, because I could have prepared myself for it with much greater success than I have. But I'm thrilled to have an exciting world to look forward to every day where the process is more important than the product, and where I no longer need to profit financially from my efforts.

The liberation that comes with aging has allowed me to get to know myself better, without fear of finding faults. I get to look and act the way I want to, without worrying about society's expectations anymore. I can more easily choose to live with my own expectations, and not too many of these, now that I'm a senior.

The only way to know is to keep our eyes open, and that means all our senses. Even then knowing may not mean knowing, but rather knowing that we don't know, and yet persisting in keeping the question alive because it is interesting and we are curious and, because, however our lives are right now, they are unfolding now, in this moment. This is truly it.

Myla and Jon Kabat-Zinn

NINETEEN

DIGNIFIED DYING

How extraordinary it is to be here at all. Awareness of death can jolt us awake to the sensuality of existence. Breath is no longer a routine inhalation of air but a quivering intake of life. The eye is quickened to the play of light and shade and color, the ear to the intricate medley of sound.

Stephen Bachelor

Buddhists tend to believe in reincarnation. If you're lucky enough to be here at all, you'll continue to be here in some form or another. Nothingness is not a choice for Buddhists. You can't get nothing out of something. You get more something.

When I was an atheist, I expected just to die and rot away in a grave somewhere, even though I don't like the idea of graves or cemeteries. Then my brother mentioned that he'd like to be cremated and have his ashes spread around Mt. Diablo. That seemed much better because it would be more ecologically sound to be interspersed with the planet. A coffin seems so isolating. But, lately, I think I'd rather have my ashes spread out in the Pacific Ocean, since I've always loved and lived near the ocean.

This atheistic expectation of death, with no afterlife, heaven or hell, or reincarnation, meant to me that whatever I was going to accomplish, I'd better do it here and now. There was no next time. I had to live in the moment. Not later, not in the past. Each moment counted.

When my mother died, I was in shock and grieved for many years. I was a grown woman of twenty-six, but that still didn't seem to matter. I was grieving for my loss and also because of the gifts my mother had given me. There could not have been a more fortunate daughter than I had been. I had been given the most loving of mothers. And I still sometimes weep over my good fortune.

Where is my mother now? I'm not entirely sure. I do know that my mother is part of me. The best part. I don't mean to say she lives on in me, but that she gave me some of herself when I was growing up, and that is now a part of me.

It's nice to think that she's somewhere up there looking out for me. But I really think she's gone on with her life at some higher level, affecting others as she affected me. I hope so.

Sometimes I think I might get to meet up with her again in my present life, with her as another entity. But I don't think that has happened.

As an educator, I expect that we learn something each time we are reincarnated and get better and better. In this, Buddhism and karma especially appeal to me. Buddhists are inclined to believe that we are reincarnated according to the karma we have earned or the ethical actions we have performed in previous lives. If we were murderers once, we may become the murdered next time. If we have achieved some degree of love and compassion once, we may be able to continue it.

All of these musings are my expectations of death. Then there's dying. I am afraid of dying. Of course. But dying is something I hope to be conscious for, no matter how painful. I don't want to miss this big event, even though I'll be more scared than ever.

I do expect to go on in some form after this life . . . better or worse, richer or poorer. The material things will matter little if I can find mindfulness to guide me.

We're all at different places on the path, which is fine. Only a very few who are enormously persistent and who take everything in life as an opportunity and not as an insult, will finally understand.

Charlotte Joko Beck

PART IV
BEYOND NOTHING

The first three sections may be instructive in themselves, but I am always left with the question—the expectation—that if I expect nothing, there must be something I can do instead, something to replace expectation with, something to hold on to—something.

Of course, there's always religion or science or mysticism, but they all involve expectations of some sort.

Let me state again that I am only a beginning Buddhist, but I think the answer is in life. Living, nature, the planet, the universe. We are all one. You are me. I am you.

TWENTY

MIRACLES

The meaning and purpose of dancing is the dance. Like music, also, it is fulfilled in each moment of its course. You do not play a sonata in order to reach the final chord, and if the meanings of things were simply in ends, composers would write nothing but finales.

Alan Watts

Human beings are made of nonhuman things. We are made of chemicals, minerals, sometimes plants and other animals, but we are always made of sunshine and rain. Without sunshine and rain there would be no life at all.

I take for granted the fact that I can read a manuscript and make sense out of it or read musical notation and sit at a keyboard and interpret it into music.

I am rarely aware of, nor would I understand, the magnificent mathematics and physics equations that are necessary for me to even move. If I see what is before me, I can translate vision into movement and reach for and get what I want. Our sensorimotor equipment is miraculous in informing us about what is available in our environment and adjusting our bodies to reach whatever goals we may set. I expect my body to work perfectly according to command, with no thought about the complicated processes involved. I am unconscious of my own miracles. The beauty of our functioning bodies is the real basis for our appreciation of beauty in ourselves and beauty in others.

I have no idea how eyes see, but I see. I have no idea how ears hear, but I hear . . . or touch or feel or move. It is magnificent how these marvels can carry on without my knowing anything about them.

I do know that our sensory systems make it possible for us to receive information from the environment and from our internal activities. These miraculous systems serve as the interface between our environment and ourselves. They interpret and translate the language of our environment into the language of our bodies—forms of energy such as sound waves or light waves are changed into electrochemical messages that go to our central nervous system and make sense out of the world for us. This world we construct is based on the information that our senses are able to perceive and transmit and translate.

The magnificence of the capacity of our parts to grow and develop in unison is another miracle. As our bones grow and elongate, so do our muscles and vessels and skin. Nothing bursts or breaks or snaps. Everything grows and develops in unison with every other element. Not only do these different parts grow simultaneously and synchronistically, but they move and bend and stretch and contract as one, with exquisite fluidity and exactitude.

We are life and living. We are seeing and sunsets and sculpture and reading. We are hearing and music and voices and bird calls. We are smelling and roses and onions and pine boughs. We are taste and chocolate and hot dogs and lobster. We are touching and hugging and feeling and loving. We are moving and running and playing and fighting.

My developing intellect grew as I experimented by acting on objects, observing the effects of those actions, and incorporating new constructs into the world of my being. In order to learn what a ball was, I had not only to look at it, but to pick it up, squeeze it, drop it, roll it on the floor, throw it in the air, bounce it up and down, throw it against a wall, drop it down a stairway, and even kick it. And I am still doing this to some extent with each new thing.

And memories. What a miracle it is to recall sunny days at the beach, the salty smell of the air as I approach the ocean, the thrill and fear as I go down a ski slope, the ideas I learned from my parents, and the joy of being with special people and doing exciting things.

And diversity. What miracles it took as life developed into multicelled beings and it became necessary for some cells to specialize in different functions to fulfill the roles required for survival. Heart cells, liver cells, brain cells, skin cells—all have the same DNA, but they learn to diversify and specialize in order to serve our needs. We all developed out of this same world. We all belong here.

Each of us is an unbelievably beautiful, meticulously designed miracle. One doesn't have to be religious or scientific to realize this. Just alive. We are God. God is us. Such a big miracle.

And yet. And yet we expect more than these miracles. We cannot seem just to be happy being alive on this miraculous planet, the way goats and cats are. We have to have something more. Some call it control, others call it progress. Some call it keeping up with the Joneses. It doesn't matter what we call it. It matters that we keep expecting more and more than the miracles we already have.

Expecting nothing means giving up control, progress, and keeping up. It means appreciating what we already have. Life is a gift.

For the human individual is not built like a car is built. He does not come into being by assembling parts, by screwing a head onto a neck, by wiring a brain into a set of lungs, or by welding veins to a heart. Head, neck, heart, lungs, brain, veins, muscles, and glands are separate names but not separate events, and these events grow into being simultaneously and interdependently. In precisely the same way, the individual is separate from his universal environment only in name.

Alan Watts

I have no idea how eyes see, but I see. I have no idea how ears hear, but I hear . . . or touch or feel or move. It is magnificent how these marvels can carry on without my knowing anything about them.

TWENTY-ONE

CHANGING

Though I can't pull Buddhism out of my back pocket and show it to you now, I think the basics of the teaching are not obscure. "Be kind, be careful, be yourself. Think before you act. Love your neighbor. Pay attention. If you are miserable, look in the mirror to find out why."
D. W. Moore

Each of us will develop different tools and different paths. As for me, I've learned the power of mindfulness and meditation. I'm still not good at either of these, as I'm still not good at expecting nothing. But this is my path.

It doesn't matter what your basic religion is. They all can work wonders. And each religion will lend itself to different likely paths, just as all of us will tend to follow our own idiosyncratic highways. All religions preach compassion and loving-kindness. How can anyone go wrong practicing these?

I am my only source for change. Regardless of my family life, socioeconomic status, age, sex, skin color, or handicaps, I can become what I am capable of becoming. One thing I am learning is that, if given a chance, knowledge, understanding, communication, and especially mindfulness lead to compassion and love. And I believe we can and must create our own evolution. We have so much to start with, so many miracles, and we can choose to create more.

Every now and then, I take risks and challenge my outer limits. Sometimes I succeed. Sometimes I don't. As I play and learn and experiment, I continue to learn laughter, wonder, and awe. I am still in the process of defining myself and changing myself. Each of us is the result of a loving and caring nature, a loving and caring planet.

But I still need to free myself from my cultural expectations and learn to appreciate myself and others without regard to body shape, size, color, sex, or ethnicity. I still need to learn to close off my vulnerabilities from the large corporations that profit from my insecurities. I still must learn to appreciate the people around me and stop analyzing their faults. I still must learn to celebrate life with all the people I meet.

We can change at any age and in any circumstance. Sometimes change is more difficult than at other times. We always have the option of more than one strategy and more than one philosophical way of interpreting our lives.

Many Buddhists have found that their primary insights come from meditation. Meditation can be extremely complex or extremely simple. Whirling dervishes probably belong in the complex category. Just keeping track of breathing in and breathing out sounds quite simple. It isn't. Our chattering minds keep finding things to solve, or worry about, or contemplate. It takes a lot of practice to stay with just breathing in and breathing out. The goal is to not have a goal. Just be fully present in whatever is happening; let go of everything else but the present moment. Meditation helps me to be mindful.

Mindfulness is about living in the here and now. I cannot be looking at expectations, comparing them with outcomes, when I am mindful.

Mindfulness is a big project. But when I am mindful I don't make mistakes. When I am here, now, and not somewhere else, I am harmonious with all around me. When I am here, now, I am fully alive.

In the past, I thought I was being efficient when I planned my teaching lesson while I drove to work. I thought I was being efficient when I did any chore faster than I had done it before. I thought I was being efficient when I rushed through each day so I could get to the end of it.

But now, when I am present, here and now in all things I am doing, I am much slower, but more precise. I rarely make mistakes. I am totally unaware of any planning going on for future projects or any rehearsal of past failures. I am attending, being present, and living each second, one at a time. When I am present here and now, I have many opportunities to learn instead of preach.

In this mindful life of awareness of everything in the here and now, I cannot have expectations because it is impossible to be expecting while I am being mindful. Expectations are a distraction from mindfulness. Mindfulness is nonjudgmental and impartial. It is impossible to take sides and still be mindful.

When I can experience life fully, patience and compassion just come naturally. If I am mindful, everyone and everything are my teachers.

Buddha said there were at least eighty-four thousand different paths. Take your choice.

Every now and then, I take risks and challenge my outer limits. Sometimes I succeed. Sometimes I don't. As I play and learn and experiment, I continue to learn laughter, wonder, and awe. I am still in the process of defining myself and changing myself. Each of us is the result of a loving and caring nature, a loving and caring planet.

REFERENCES

PAGE

xi. Richard Baker, "Notes on the Practice and Territory of the Precepts," in Thich Nhat Hanh, *For a Future To Be Possible: Commentaries on the Five Wonderful Precepts,* Berkeley, CA: Parallax Press, 1993, p. 148.

xiii. Pema Chodron, *The Wisdom of No Escape and the Path of Loving-Kindness,* Boston: Shambhala, 1991, p. 30.

3. Sogyal Rinpoche, *The Tibetan Book of Living and Dying,* San Francisco: Harper San Francisco, 1994, p. 57.

5. _____, *ibid.*, p. 62.

11. Dalai Lama and Phil Borges, *Tibetan Portrait: The Power of Compassion*, New York: Rizzoli, 1996, p. 3.

13. Alan Watts, *The Book*, New York: Vintage, 1966, p. 6.

15. Rachel Carson, *A Sense of Wonder*, New York: Harper and Row, 1957, p. 21.

17. Matthew Fox, *A Spirituality Named Compassion*, San Francisco: HarperSanFrancisco, 1979, p. 167.

19. _____, *ibid.*, p. 167.

21. Thich Nhat Hanh, *For a Future To Be Possible: Commentaries on the Five Wonderful Precepts*, Berkeley, CA: Parallax Press, 1993, p. 99.

23. Peter Matthiessen, *Nine-Headed Dragon River*, Boston: Shambhala, 1998, p. 76.

25. Matthew Fox, *A Spirituality Named Compassion*, San Francisco: HarperSanFrancisco, 1979, p. 72.

28. Dalai Lama and Phil Borges, *Tibetan Portrait: The Power of Compassion*, New York: Rizzoli, 1996, p. 40.

33. *The Anguttura Mikaya,* translated by F. L. Woodward and E. M. Hare, in Jack Kornfield (ed.) *The Teachings of Buddha,* Boston: Shambhala, 1996, p. 119.

35. Matthew Fox, *A Spirituality Named Compassion,* San Francisco: HarperSanFrancisco, 1979, p. xi.

37. Myla and Jon Kabat-Zinn, *Everyday Blessings: The Inner Work of Mindful Parenting,* New York: Hyperion, 1997, p. 328.

40. George Bernard Shaw, in Jack Canfield's *Chicken Soup for the Soul,* Deerfield Beach, FL: Health Communications, 1993, p. 83.

43. Jack Kornfield, "The Practice of Meditation," in Jeffrey Mishlove, *Thinking Aloud: Conversations on the Leading Edge of Knowledge,* Tulsa: Council Oaks Books, 1992, pp. 304–312.

45. Peter Matthiessen, *Nine-Headed Dragon River,* Boston: Shambhala, 1998, p. 95.

47. Pema Chodron, *The Wisdom of No Escape and the Path of Loving-Kindness,* Boston: Shambhala, 1991, p. 33.

48. *The Sutta Nipata,* translated by K. R. Norman, in *The Group Discourses,* London: The Pali Text Society, 1984, p. 101.

51. Dainin Katagiri, *Returning to Silence: Zen Practice in Daily Life,* Boston: Shambhala, 1988, p. 15.

54. D. W. Moore, *The Accidental Buddhist: Mindfulness, Enlightenment, and Sitting Still,* Chapel Hill, NC: Algonquin Books of Chapel Hill, 1997, p. 190.

57. Myla and Jon Kabat-Zinn, *Everyday Blessings: The Inner Work of Mindful Parenting,* New York: Hyperion, 1997, p. 311.

59. John Fitzgerald Kennedy, *Inaugural Address,* January 20, 1961.

61. Henryk Skolinowski, "New thought, new world," *VIEW,* No. 9, 1997, San Francisco: Rigpa Publications, p. 19.

64. Herryman Mauer, *The Way of Ways: Lao Tzu/Tao Teh Ching,* New York: Schocken Books, 1985, p. 7.

67. Charlotte Joko Beck, *Nothing Special: Living Zen,* New York: HarperCollins, 1993, p. 53.

69. John Fitzgerald Kennedy, Press Conference, March 21, 1962.

73. Joseph Pearce, *Exploring the Crack in the Cosmic Egg,* New York: The Julian Press, 1974, p. 4.

80. Pema Chodron, *Start Where You Are: A guide to compassionate living,* Boston: Shambhala, 1994, p. 4.

83. Thich Nhat Hanh, *Peace Is Every Step,* New York: Bantam, 1991, p. 8.

87. Dalai Lama and Phil Borges, *Tibetan Portrait: The Power of Compassion,* New York: Rizzoli, 1996, p. 26.

90. *The Dhammapada: The Sayings of Buddha,* translated by Thomas Byrom, New York: Alfred A. Knopf, 1976, p. 4.

93. Pema Chodron, *The Wisdom of No Escape and the Path of Loving-Kindness,* Boston: Shambhala, 1991, p. 26.

95. Charlotte Joko Beck, *Everyday Zen: Love and Work,* San Francisco: Harper San Francisco, 1989, p. v.

97. Myla and Jon Kabat-Zinn, *Everyday Blessings: The Inner Work of Mindful Parenting,* New York: Hyperion, 1997, p. 339.

99. Stephen Bachelor, *Buddhism Without Beliefs,* New York: Riverhead Books, 1997, p. 32.

101. Charlotte Joko Beck, *Nothing Special: Living Zen,* New York: HarperCollins, 1993, p. 127.

105. Alan Watts, *The Wisdom of Insecurity*, New York: Vintage, 1957, p. 116.

108. _____, *The Book*, New York: Vintage, 1966, p. 64.

111. D. W. Moore, *The Accidental Buddhist: Mindfulness, Enlightenment, and Sitting Still*, Chapel Hill, NC: Algonquin Books of Chapel Hill, 1997, p. 101.

ALSO AVAILABLE FROM

TUTTLE PUBLISHING

Buddhism Plain and Simple
by Steve Hagen

To Know Yourself, To Know Zen
by Albert Low

Instant Zen
by Jim McMullan

Simple Buddhism
by C. Alexander Simpkins Ph.D. and Annellen Simpkins Ph.D.

Simple Zen
by C. Alexander Simpkins Ph.D. and Annellen Simpkins Ph.D.

Zen and the Beat Way
by Alan Watts

Zen Around the World
by C. Alexander Simpkins Ph.D. and Annellen Simpkins Ph.D.

Zen Flesh, Zen Bones
by Paul Reps

Zen Meditation Plain and Simple
by Albert Low